GPS to Joy Workbook

Maryl Petreccia

GPS to Joy
Companion Workbook

Introducing
THE JOY ACTIVATION PROCESS
Technology

GPS to Joy Companion Workbook

Introducing: THE JOY ACTIVATION PROCESS
Technology

Published by KDP

A Joyful Life Series

Copyright © 2021

ISBN: 978-0-9600013-1-6

Cover design and interior compass and wave art by Jim Saurbaugh, JS Graphic Design

GPS to Joy Workbook

Maryl Petreccia

GPS to Joy
Companion Workbook

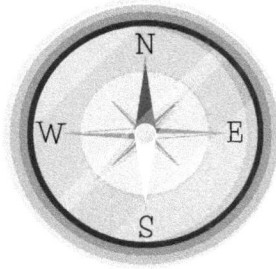

Introducing
THE JOY ACTIVATION PROCESS
Technology

GPS to Joy Workbook

Table of Contents

Welcome, *joy seekers...*

I'm so happy to be connected with you here! You probably know me and my story if you are holding this workbook. But in case you don't, I'm Maryl Petreccia and guiding people back to joy and all that includes is my jam, my life purpose. My official title per my marketing guru: I'm a Mid-life Transition Coach but my superpower is being your Personal Power Catalyst.

What a privilege to be doing a JOY deep dive with you!

If I asked you how this book fell into your hands, I hope it's because your soul is screaming "give me a joy overhaul ASAP!" And you're ready to generate that "better than I could even imagine!" kind of joy. But, it's also possible that you've recently experienced a "no-going-back" life alteration that has knocked you off of your center. Now, you're feeling stuck, like you've had a serious setback and you're feeling super vulnerable all at the same time. Wherever you are on the Joy Continuum^R journey, I get it. Maybe it will make you feel better to know that this is a universal right of passage for everyone over the age of 10! All of us, at some point, find ourselves at that same starting place before the doors of joy reopen. And that puts us square in that annoyingly familiar/unfamiliar **unknown**. And if your life has *really* been blown up, then you likely are at a loss on how to approach navigating your life re-launch because it feels like there are either way too many options or NO options at all.

Your head is spinning because you don't know which way to turn! Sweetness, I want to give you some peace of mind here. Used well, this could be one of the biggest adventures of your life!

I realize that many of you have been hit really hard and you have my heart! There's no denying that the world has been in a state of turmoil and chaos that's put everything in a collective talespin. Some of my clients felt devastated when they lost their home base...either someone special died or they endured a divorce or a devastating break-up.

My VIP client, Marina, had a seriously mind-numbing year. In the blink of an eye, her body was thrown into menopause, she faced an empty nest as a single mom, and retired as a bank manager with no plan B. She was blown over by the giant tsunami of major life transitions. After we spent time remapping her future, she quickly turned those transitions on their heads!

We took our time (why rush this juicy process?) and tapped her back into her personal power, using THE JOY ACTIVATION PROCESS technology to do a deep dive into her JOY gap and discover what she needed to do to close it. She's physically feeling better than ever thanks to her new nutrition and health routine, she got active with her friends playing in a pickleball league and is now pursuing her dream of writing romance novels while studying to be a travel agent for single women travelers over 50. She's nailing it!

Wherever you are in your joy journey, the stars that you once used to navigate your life seem to have disappeared from your sky. Your struggle to imagine what's next for you is real BECAUSE the unknown has no preset coordinates. They need your direction. That fact can test your patience and forget about your hope and confidence for a joy-driven tomorrow.

Honey, I get it.

This workbook is a companion to my book *GPS to Joy* which I wrote to tell my own story of loss and transitions and to help you navigate life's turbulence and toughest transitions to find your new direction.

I found myself on the most heart-wrenching journey in my life when my husband was diagnosed with brain cancer and died the following year. As I stumbled to the other side of the grief for what seemed like eternity and eventually saw light and joy again, friends asked me how I did it. So I stopped and reflected about how I alchemized the pain and losses turning all of that back into a profoundly deep experience of joy. As I poured my process onto paper, THE JOY ACTIVATION PROCESS was born. Although it took alot of inner work (the good kind), I'm living proof that it works and I mean REALLY works.

Use this workbook on your own, with me leading a class, with me as a VIP client, or as an accompaniment while reading *GPS to Joy*. It's your call. Make this book your own. Doodle in it, write down favorite words on the inside cover, or add some stickers. Perhaps you want to pick out a special pen that you keep clipped to the cover. Even though we may be treading through some rough waters, let this experience be fun and light. You are treating yourself to a deep dive! If any of the questions or prompts are too big right now, blow past them and return to them later. Make this process as enjoyable as possible! Light a candle, turn on music, and give yourself this luxe time and focus.

However you are thinking about using this workbook, the best way I know to have it do it's magic is for you to take on each module of questions, then go out and apply the lessons in your world for at least a week in between each module. Give yourself the time! Personal growth that sticks isn't meant to happen overnight. As with anything you value, it won't be painless or tearless, however it won't be rudderless. Growth and change are organic processes that meet you where you are and really does need your full participation. Staying "safely" on the sidelines as a curious observer (without applying what you discover) won't close your gap. If there's a time that you'd love a little (or a lot) of support, you can always DM me on instagram or contact me via my website www.marylpetreccia.com.

So, let's take a look at what lies ahead in this workbook!

QUESTIONS - that unfold for you where you are right now. I have figured out that you move forward most powerfully when you know where the starting line is. You've heard the quote, "you can move what you measure." That applies to joy too!

PRACTICES - that let YOU learn more about YOU and invite new stuff (new contexts, new concepts, new mindsets, and new possibilities) in your life.

TAKE ACTION - daily actions assignments and journal prompts to ground your discoveries and reinforce your new normal to solidify the new you and turn all of this from a journey into a grand adventure!

This book is laid out to cover 12 weeks, for you to do questions and practices over the 7 days, with a new journal prompt each day. I would love for you to dive in and work on it as closely to this format as possible. The most important thing is to complete the book, even if it takes a year. Commit to yourself, commit to your healing process, commit to this book.

Now take this book, grab your favorite writing utensil, your favorite beverage, and let's roll!

Module 1

Getting Grounded....With Gratitude

> *"We have to embrace obstacles to reach the next stage of joy."*
>
> —*Goldie Hawn*

The word "grounded" means different things depending on the context. On the bright side, it can mean that you are well balanced and sensible. But grounded has a shadow side and for many of us, that refers to the experience of feeling stuck, like a plane that just can't fly because it's grounded because there's something that's not safe about it. When we bring light to those matters, thoughts and feelings that keep us down, and stuck, it's there that we can dig a bit and see emotions that need releasing.

My client, Ava had a boss who was stressed and exploded at his staff more times than she could count. She was exhausted by it. When she came to me for coaching, we took our time to understand that the situation was toxic and it was impacting her life on many fronts. Once we did a deep dive on the entire dynamic and situation, she began to see that she had choices about navigating herself in a more empowered way. Of course, she could remain in that toxic work relationship and speak to HR or directly with him. But she also realized that she could find something else that served her. She needed to release her fears and bring her wisdom to the blueprint we crafted for her. She grounded her thinking in what would empower her and bring her joy in her work. Once she freed herself from the erroneous belief that she had no safe options, she tapped into her personal power and executed the blueprint. Today, she's happy working as a solopreneur as a special accounting consultant. She's clear on her ideal client and works only with people that she likes, that value her personally and professionally and that inspire her. She lives inside the context that her work brings her fulfillment and joy.

Just a note...if you choose to remain in a toxic or less than optimal relationship from fear, there is a bridge beyond the fear that shows up for you to cross when you focus on higher energetics such as fulfillment, satisfaction and joy. If you see yourself suffering, you are navigating away from joy. **Let this be your time to be free!**

Even though fear is part of life, navigating toward joy asks that you release yourself from any negative anchors in your life that keep you grounded by the shadows.

QUESTIONS

Answer the questions below. Take your time with them. Come back to them throughout the next few days and weeks. You are in a spot where you need to rebuild your foundation. We build solid foundations by ensuring that the terrain is safe and solid. It might be a rocky trip at first, but you will get there and be better for it on the other side.

Be brave. Be honest. Be true to yourself.

1) Describe the issue that is challenging you:

   The issue I'm dealing with is: (*Example:* *I can't find the relationship I want.*)

   _____

   _____

_____

_____

_____

2) What is stopping you from feeling joy? Guilt, obligations, feeling stuck, other people, financials? List them all.

_____

_____

_____

_____

_____

_____

_____

_____

_____

3) What would make your life extraordinary?

_____

_____

_____

_____

_____

_____

_____

4) What parts of your life need immediate attention?

_____

_____

_____

_____

_____

_____

_____

_____

_____

5) What parts of your life have you been putting on the back burner?

_____

_____

_____

_____

_____

_____

_____

_____

_____

_____

Now to the "practice makes progress" section.

At the end of each module, you will find a **"Take Action"** section. These actions are for you to practice or observe daily and to journal about. Even if you jot down an idea or quick sentence or two acknowledging and observing what you do and what happens when you take action, that's perfectly fine. Some days you might find yourself filling up several pages, and that is ok, too. I will provide places to write, but feel free to write more in your own journal or in the back of this book as needed. Also, there are prompt questions, as an option to continue your reflections. Use them if they speak to you. . Most importantly, plug into your feelings and reactions. Try your best to do these every day. It might feel a bit awkward at first, but power through. As you do it, it gets easi*er.*

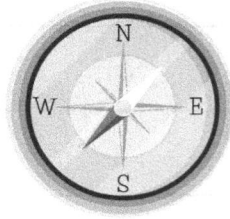

TAKE ACTION - Week One:

Every time you have a knee-jerk reaction or negative reaction to something, I encourage you **not** to indulge the negativity. Instead flip your thoughts.

Here's a real time, personal example of what I mean. I was just at Dallas airport and got so distracted between flights that when I returned to the gate, the airline staffer at the counter refused my boarding since I missed the boarding cut-off time. I got booked on another flight 3 hours later. At that moment, I refused to get angry with the airline or myself for missing the boarding time. Instead, I took a deep breath and let it be, took ownership that I missed the timing and that all was well, then focused on editing my new book as I waited for the next flight. When I think back to the moment, I CHANGED MY FOCUS by not allowing my thoughts to change my state of mind and bring me down. I have this suggestion for you. Why not tell yourself that you did all you had the capacity to do in that moment? Love that you had the ability to do as much as you did and tell the negative thought to scram. Then, do something joyful like think of a joyful moment (think eating your favorite ice cream or watching a gorgeous sunset, or even your special first kiss...anything that fills you with joy). If you start with building the habit of having joy-filled thoughts overpower knee-jerk reactions, you'll recalibrate your GPS toward joy and away from the negative.

Do this for a week and make notes about times and places these knee-jerk reactions come out.

Day 1 Journaling: What knee-jerk reactions did you have today, and how did you flip your thoughts to be positive?

_____

_____

_____

_____

_____

_____

_____

Day 2 Journaling: What were the knee-jerks today? How were they different from yesterday?

_____

_____

_____

_____

_____

_____

_____

_____

_____

_____

_____

Day 3 Journaling: What were the knee-jerks today? Are they getting easier to spot?

_____

_____

_____

_____

_____

_____

_____

_____

_____

_____

_____

_____

_____

Day 4 Journaling: What were the knee-jerks today? How were they different from yesterday?

_____

_____

_____

_____

_____

_____

_____

_____

_____

_____

Day 5 Journaling: What were the knee-jerks today? Are there more or less than the beginning of the week and how do you feel about that?

_____

_____

_____

_____

_____

_____

_____

_____

_____

_____

_____

Day 6 Journaling: What were the knee-jerks today? Is the positivity replacement getting easier or harder and why?

_____

_____

_____

_____

_____

_____

_____

_____

_____

_____

_____

_____

Day 7 Journaling: What were the knee-jerks today? Do you feel like you are harder on yourself today, or on day one of this exercise?

_____

_____

_____

_____

_____

_____

_____

_____

_____

You've made it to the end of week one! Remember the first step is the hardest, and you did it! The next hardest step is to keep going. For a bonus breathing activity to help keep you centered, go to www.marylpetreccia.com/workbookbonus

Maryl Petreccia

Module 2

Straying from Joy: Your Joy Tank on Empty

"Sometimes a simple shift in perspective is all you need to refocus your time and energy on what's important."

-Melanie Benson

Imagine you're having a conversation with joy.

Hi, you! This is Joy talking. I've missed you! We always had so much fun together. I miss the sound of your laughter, the way you would dance in circles with your head back and your arms spread wide. We were tight! Two peas in a pod. What happened to you? Where did you go? I'm still here. The last time I saw you, we were playing hide and seek. I hid. And waited…I'm still waiting. Why haven't you come back? Are you ready to keep playing? Are you hiding too? I promise I'll come take your hand when you call, 'Olly olly oxen free'!

Joy hasn't abandoned us, but through our turbulence and life's tough transitions, it's easy to forget joy. When that happens, it can feel like joy tanks are simply sputtering on empty.

This module is all about joy and filling up your joy tank. This might seem like a pendulum swing from last week, however, there's no time like the present to start practicing putting joy and positivity back into our daily lives.

Depending on where you are in your journey, this might feel gratuitous, like you don't deserve to do that right now. Let nothing stop you! Not guilt, shame, doubt, or anything else. Flowers need sunshine to grow. You need happiness and warmth to do the same. Joy is not a crime; quite the opposite. I say cultivating joy is our obligation to ourselves, our families and our future. You need joy. You deserve joy. The world and your family is better when you are plugged into your joy. Now, let's go and fill up your joy tank!

QUESTIONS

1) In *GPS to Joy* I say "think of joy as child's play." What are some things you want to do or are currently doing that bring a feeling of joy to your life?

_____

_____

_____

_____

_____

2) What would bring more joy and give you a better life than what you have now?

_____

_____

_____

_____

_____

_____

_____

_____

3) What would you need to say goodbye to right now so that joy can emerge?

_____

_____

_____

_____

_____

_____

_____

_____

4) Are you willing to address the issues that take your joy away?

_____

_____

_____

_____

_____

_____

_____

_____

_____

_____

5) What is an activity you like doing or something you like watching? Go do or watch that thing, or even simply imagine yourself doing that now. Let it sink in and notice...where do you feel the joy in your body? What other emotions do you feel? Do you feel any guilt in doing this activity?

_____

_____

_____

_____

_____

_____

_____

_____

_____

_____

PRACTICES

This section has optional practices to invoke more joy. For you poets, write a poem. For those of you who love art, draw a picture or make a collage. For you song birds and songwriters, create music and musical words.

Take a few minutes and notice...what are the sensations that you feel when you feel joy? Butterflies? Weak in the knees, tension releasing from your shoulders, feeling heat in your cheeks?

CREATE AN IMAGE

Label where you experience joy in your body:

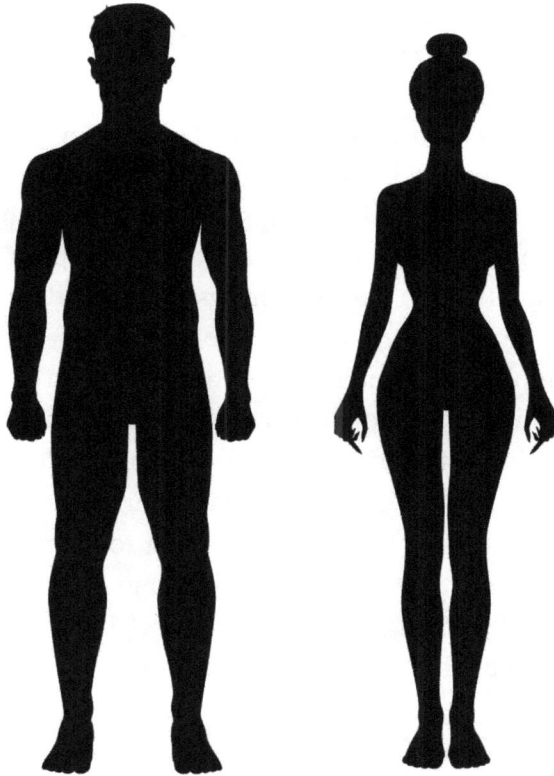

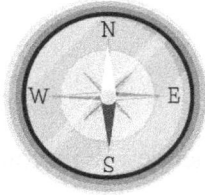

TAKE ACTION - Week Two:

As I wrote in chapter two of *GPS to Joy,* joy exists in all the realms of our lives. Take time to look around each day. Find joy in at least five things. Example: Use this affirmation - "Every glass of water I drink helps to purify my body into optimal health and that brings me joy." Use this affirmation for work. "My job is a great teacher. Whether I love it completely or see myself moving beyond it soon, it sustains my livelihood so I can meet my needs and the needs of my family. I am grateful that I can contribute my talents. That brings me joy!" As for friends, "Friends who seem pushy or question my choices care enough to share their viewpoints. Anything that pushes me gives me strength and I can love them for loving me enough to care. Their commitment to my happiness brings me joy!"

Please come up with 3 affirmations of your own right now that acknowledge joy.

1. _____

2. _____

_____

3. _____

_____

Utilize these affirmations in different areas of your life for a week and reflect about them each day and what joy you can find in them.

For inspiration or to see my affirmations head to www.gpstojoybook.com/bonuses to find my personal daily affirmations.

Day 1 Journaling: What are some simple joys that you experienced today? Smells? Tastes? Feelings?

_____

_____

_____

_____

_____

_____

_____

_____

_____

_____

_____

Day 2 Journaling: What are 3 of the most difficult things in your life? Time to reframe them! What joy can be found in each one?

_____

_____

_____

_____

_____

_____

_____

_____

_____

_____

_____

_____

Day 3 Journaling: What were the joys today? How were they different from yesterday?

_____

_____

_____

_____

_____

_____

_____

_____

_____

_____

_____

Mid-Week BONUS Fun!

Go out and actively find and do one thing that gives you joy. For me it's making a cup of hot tea, getting a massage, or going for a hike during sunset. Find and do one thing every day, and take all the pleasure in for yourself!

Day 4 Journaling: What were the joys today? Are they getting easier to identify?

_____

_____

_____

_____

_____

_____

_____

_____

Day 5 Journaling: What were the joys today? Are they harder to see than the beginning of the week? How do you feel about that?

_____

_____

_____

_____

_____

_____

_____

_____

_____

_____

Day 6 Journaling: What were the joys today? Is the positivity replacement getting easier or harder and why?

_____

_____

_____

_____

_____

_____

_____

_____

_____

_____

_____

Day 7 Journaling: Go back to basic joys like wind on your face, the first sip of your favorite beverage, or the hug from someone you haven't seen in a while. List five of them and how each one makes you feel.

_____

_____

_____

_____

_____

_____

_____

_____

_____

_____

Module 2: For inspiration or to see my affirmations head to www.marylpetreccia.com/workbookbonus to find my personal daily affirmations.

Module 3

Replacing Habits that get us Off Course

"Let your joy be in your journey—not in some distant goal."
- Tim Cook

I still have knee-jerk reactions in the back of my overachieving mind like *I could have done more, been more, given more,* but I do my best to not indulge them. Experiencing joy has now replaced my previous thirst for adrenaline. In fact, joy is my new baseline. As part and parcel to that, I create intentions, embrace visions for how my life unfolds, and I experience dreams consciously fulfilled. In other words, I manifest and materialize my dreams and visions. But this is part of the process that has a prerequisite called letting go of the shadow sides of our reactions and loving our future by connecting with joy.

My capacity to bring intention and compassion to even the toughest experiences allowed for more love than suffering. I created joy as I was able. Rather than avoiding the painful emotions, I made room for all of the emotions that arose for all of us in dealing with death, without judgment of anyone, including myself.

QUESTIONS

1) When you're in a crisis, what are your go-to habits? What do you see as positive and what do you see as negative?

_____

_____

_____

_____

_____

2) What is compassion to you? Define it and give examples. Do you practice these?

_____

_____

_____

_____

_____

3) Do you let yourself trust and rely on others? Why or why not?

_____

_____

_____

_____

4) What are your strengths? How do you use and access them all?

_____

_____

_____

_____

_____

PRACTICES

Create a mantra, one that will help you focus and stay strong (My favorite is: I am unlimited!). Write one here, and on a sticky note, and keep it on your bedside table, your fridge, or your bathroom mirror and repeat it daily.

_____

_____

_____

_____

_____

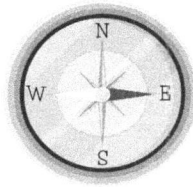

TAKE ACTION - Week Three:

Bringing intention and compassion to even the toughest experiences allows for more love than suffering. Rather than avoid the painful emotions, make room for all of the emotions that arise without judgment of anyone, including yourself.

This week, look for compassion. Replace negativity, anger, or judgement with compassion. At the end of the week, I'd like you to look at what changes you experience and feel when you flip that switch.

Day 1 Journaling: What did you notice today as you stepped into more compassion?

_____

_____

_____

_____

_____

_____

_____

_____

_____

_____

_____

_____

Day 2 Journaling: What, for you, is currently the most difficult thing about being compassionate?

_____

_____

_____

_____

_____

_____

_____

_____

_____

_____

_____

_____

Day 3 Journaling: What, for you, is easy about being compassionate?

_____

_____

_____

_____

_____

_____

_____

_____

_____

_____

_____

_____

Mid-Week BONUS fun!

Uplevel your energy by expanding your generosity! Do something nice for someone with the intention of expanding your heart. Call someone you've been meaning to have a good chat with, take a friend to lunch, or buy a stranger coffee.

Day 4 Journaling: Is compassion worth the feelings you are getting in return?

_____

_____

_____

_____

_____

_____

_____

_____

Day 5 Journaling: Is it getting easier or harder to be compassionate?

Day 6 Journaling: What happened the last time you fell back into your former habit and lost your compassion connection?

_____

_____

_____

_____

_____

_____

_____

_____

_____

Day 7 Journaling: Go back to thinking an unforgiving thought today toward yourself and someone else. How does that feel now in your body?

_____

_____

_____

_____

_____

_____

_____

_____

_____

_____

You've made it to the end of week three! Breaking habits is the way to navigate to a new life. For a bonus on breaking bad habits, go to www.gpstojoybook.com/bonuses

Module 4

Plotting New Coordinates

> *"Nothing comes ahead of its time, and nothing has ever happened that didn't need to happen."*
>
> *-Byron Katie*

It's time to start plotting new coordinates to get busy navigating your joy. If you're reluctant to reposition your life—to find new stars by which to guide your own course—I get that. That happened to me too.

The thing to remember is that you have two choices:

1. Remain stalled and outside of your zone of JOY.
2. Plot new coordinates and choose to become the best joy navigator you can be!

This all starts with relaxing, breathing, letting go where you're feeling tight, and getting beyond what you can see otherwise known as going beyond your previous line of sight. When you let go of the past, you can course correct to a joyful future. Consider the idea that your roles have changed, and so has where you are headed, so it's time to discover your new true north.

QUESTIONS

1) What are the biggest expectations of you right now and from whom?

_____

_____

_____

_____

_____

2) What do you feel like you fail at, miserably?

_____

_____

_____

_____

_____

_____

3) What is your evidence that you have failed?

_____

_____

_____

_____

_____

4) What do you say to yourself when facing something you believe that you failed at?

_____

_____

_____

_____

_____

_____

5) What would you need to be free of or free from to move forward? What would it take to feel liberated into your zone of Joy?

_____

_____

_____

_____

_____

PRACTICES

Write a sad story about something you failed at. (It doesn't have to be long.)

_____

_____

_____

_____

_____

Now, reframe it by writing a happy story about the same thing you failed at.

_____

_____

_____

_____

_____

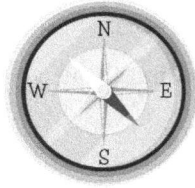

TAKE ACTION - Week Four:

Taking action to create your new course in life isn't for the weary of heart because it puts us square inside the "unknown." But you're not weary and I will show you how to make friends with the unknown. Actually, most great journeys start without knowing the ending. In fact, once you start your new course you most likely will change your direction. And that is ok. Whether you are unclear or know exactly where you're going, the activity below will help you gain the clarity you need to plot new coordinates with intention.

Day 1 Journaling: What did you dream of being as a kid and what do you LOVE to do? (These can be ANYTHING. Don't judge. Just write.)

_____

_____

_____

Day 2 Journaling: What is the most difficult or biggest goal you've achieved in your life so far?

_____

_____

_____

_____

_____

_____

_____

_____

_____

_____

_____

Day 3 Journaling: When else in your life did you change course, direction, or focus in your life?

_____

_____

_____

_____

_____

_____

_____

_____

_____

_____

_____

_____

Day 4 Journaling: Name one goal you would like to achieve now and map out the steps to get there. (Example: I want a promotion at work. I need to finish this big project I'm working on now, create a proposal or talking points as to why I should be promoted, get a meeting with my boss, and affirm my worth).

_____

_____

_____

_____

_____

_____

_____

_____

_____

_____

Day 5 Journaling: What is the hardest thing about a new goal for you?

_____

_____

_____

_____

_____

_____

_____

_____

_____

_____

_____

Day 6 Journaling: What are the things holding you back?

_____

_____

_____

_____

_____

_____

_____

_____

_____

_____

_____

_____

Day 7 Journaling: Think of a small goal that you could achieve in a day. (Examples: Cleaning out a closet, putting something together, finishing a book.) Go do that and write how you feel after completing the task.

_____

_____

_____

_____

_____

_____

_____

_____

_____

_____

BONUS ACTIVITY

Fill in the smallest steps to map out your plan for accomplishing what you wrote on Day 4. Go even smaller. Think of some of the steps as rocks, some as pebbles, and these steps might be sand.

For example, if you want to tackle a mountain of paperwork, Let's not talk about how big it's gotten because it's terrible. Unfortunately, every time you think about it, you feel overwhelmed and conveniently find something else to do.

What's the tiniest first step? Sort the paperwork by category.

_____

_____

_____

_____

_____

_____

_____

_____

So, what is the absolute lowest bar you can set for yourself?
What is the tiniest first step you can take?

_____

_____

_____

_____

_____

_____

_____

_____

Module 5

Filling your Joy Tank

"The more the heart is sated with joy, the more it becomes insatiable."

- Gabrielle Roy

Joy is always inviting its presence and is available to experience. It is not forced. Choice and attitude is our access to joy. Our willingness to have joy is also a must. Living in your zone of joy is much more powerful than being focused on controlling, commanding, or forcing anything.

C.S. Lewis wrote, "Real joy seems to me almost as unlike security or prosperity as it is unlike agony.... It jumps under one's ribs and tickles down one's back and makes one forget meals and keeps one (delightedly) sleepless o' nights. It shocks one awake when the other puts one to sleep. My private table is one second of joy and is worth 12 hours of pleasure.

"Joy (in my sense) has indeed one characteristic, and one only, in common with them; the fact that anyone who has experienced it will want it again.... I doubt whether anyone who has tasted it would ever, if both were in his power, exchange it for all the pleasures in the world."

The great thing about joy is that more joy begets more joy! Even for those moments where you feel like you're forcing it, joy has a funny way of entering your being and invites more joy! So what are you waiting for?

QUESTIONS

1) What inspires you?

_____

_____

_____

_____

_____

_____

_____

2) How often do you fall into the martyr habit where you put others first at your own expense? Name a few examples (if you feel more comfortable make-up names or write nicknames):

_____

_____

_____

_____

_____

3) What would make your life extraordinary? Make a list, write prose, draw...whatever moves you.

_____

_____

_____

_____

_____

_____

_____

_____

_____

4) Look out at the people in your life. What are they doing that brings them joy? What are you envious of? (This is a great way to spot what you desire and don't yet have sorted out.)

_____

_____

_____

_____

_____

5) Where are you amazing as a human? What is valued about you?

_____

_____

_____

_____

_____

_____

PRACTICES

Create a "you" space. Find things that you treasure including awards or things that remind you of how you are appreciated. Put them in a spot in your house that you walk by a lot.

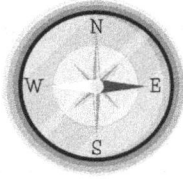

TAKE ACTION - Week Five:

Get ready to step into your joy zone! This is a week of fun and finding the inner you. It might feel weird, crazy, or just not "you," but remember *joy is right below the surface*! Do your best, even if it feels weird or foreign; these are your inner conflicts and resistances. Don't let them call the shots.

Day 1 Journaling: How do you feel every time you walk past the "you space" you created?

_____

_____

_____

_____

_____

_____

_____

_____

_____

_____

_____

Day 2 Journaling: Draw something. Anything. It doesn't have to be good. Bonus points if you use multiple colors or mediums.

Day 3 Journaling: How did you feel while you colored yesterday at the beginning? At the end?

_____

_____

_____

_____

_____

Day 4 Journaling: Put on your favorite song (old or new) and dance to the whole song. As big and as crazy as you want! How do you feel after? Did you jump in right away? Did it take time to get started?

_____

_____

_____

_____

Day 5 Journaling: Compliment someone in real life. Even if you have to pick up the phone to do so. How did they react? How did it make you feel?

Day 6 Journaling: Plan out an imaginary dinner party for three of your favorite people. Give the party a theme. What would the theme be and what kind of food would you have? Who would you invite? Where would the location be? How would you decorate? Would you bring out the china and fancy stemware?

_____

_____

_____

_____

Day 7 Journaling: Make a special place for you in your home. Maybe it's a comfy chair, pillows on the floor, or the perfect view. Make a favorite beverage and sit there doing nothing but enjoying your drink for thirty minutes. Write about how you feel while sitting in this place.

_____

_____

_____

_____

_____

_____

_____

_____

_____

_____

_____

_____

_____

For a bonus on joy and the Joy Activation Process, go to www.gpstojoybook.com/bonuses

Module 6

Finding Joy in getting clarity around your Finances

"Find joy in everything you choose to do. Every job, relationship, home… it's your responsibility to love it, or change it."
                                                            - Chuck Palahniuk

I have found there's joy in developing compassionate and practical practices for having financial finesse! After 30 years of doing this, I am now semi-retired. I purchased another home, and now have passive income investments.

All of this happened by shifting how I saved and spent, and how I took responsibility for my financial life. I found joy in growing my ability to navigate finances into abundance.

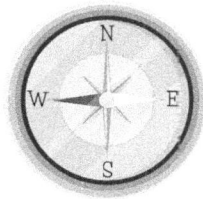

TAKE ACTION - Week Six:

Buckle up. This week is a bit bumpy if you've never really looked at your financial situation objectively. But clarity liberates, and gaining clarity on your current situation is the first step in creating and mapping out a financial plan that will propel you on a new course.

QUESTIONS

Day 1 Journaling: What do you currently see as your biggest financial hurdles?

_____

_____

_____

_____

_____

_____

_____

Day 2 Journaling: Where does your money currently come from? Take a few minutes to list out your sources of income. Don't worry, you can always go back and make any needed changes. Now, list out your outflows. Where is your money going? Be as brutally accurate as you can be by accounting for every dollar. No one is judging here.

_____

_____

_____

_____

_____

_____

_____

_____

_____

_____

Day 3 Journaling: What are your three top financial goals?
What do you want? Think REALLY big. What do you dream
of for yourself? Nothing is too big or small. This is about
you saying what YOU want and what you dream of.
Examples: money in savings, a special trip, a down payment
for a home, so much spending money per month.

_____

_____

_____

_____

_____

_____

_____

_____

_____

Day 4 Journaling: I highly suggest reading the following article about FINANCIAL FREEDOM and LITERACY.

"What Do You Need to Know About Financial Literacy?" found on www.ramseysolutions.com

I also love The Rachel Cruze Show on YouTube. She makes learning about finances simple, not stressful. Her advice is full of wisdom and shows how to make real progress toward your goals. www.youtube.com/RachelCruze

Take some time to discern three actions you could take that would move your financial dreams and wants forward.

_____

_____

_____

_____

_____

_____

_____

Day 5 Journaling: Visioning Your Success. Take a moment and imagine. Financially, where are you in 10 years? Journal what you are imagining in the present tense as if you are looking at your life in the future. How you will get there doesn't matter. Get juicy with the details! This is the most important exercise of the week.

_____

_____

_____

_____

_____

_____

_____

_____

_____

_____

Day 6 Journaling: Take a moment to describe how the most important people in your life will benefit from the vision you just created for the future you. What will your life together look like? How are you enjoying and celebrating your abundance? Be sure to include those things that will remain the same so you bridge your future with the things you love to have with you always.

_____

_____

_____

_____

_____

_____

_____

_____

_____

_____

Day 7 Journaling: As your next action, set an appointment to talk to a financial advisor about a consultation on how to manage and invest for your wants and dreams to be realized. (They're usually free.) Journal how you feel after talking to this person or if you haven't talked to them yet, how does it feel to have that appointment set?

_____

_____

_____

_____

_____

_____

_____

_____

_____

Module 7

The Joy Scale

"Find a place inside where there's joy, and the joy will burn out the pain."

- Joseph Campbell

Life's defining moments or disruptions, you know, those unforgettable moments that permanently change the course of our lives, are what I call transitions.

Others call them losses or passages. Whatever you call them, they share some common features. First, we often don't see them coming. Second, they are definitely life-altering. Third, they hit us hard like a tidal wave, a blow so potent that nothing we know to be true seems to remain in its aftermath.

With the old terrain gone, we are left completely exposed, dazed, and blinded in our ability to see what's next. Only then can transformation begin.

Joy has a wide spectrum—it can come spontaneously, and it can be sustained. Sustained joy needs more from us. We must activate it by becoming more aware of what's true for us, connecting to that truth, and by simple practice.

THE JOY SCALE

Please fill in the scale and see where you stand today. Feel free to compare your results from before if you did this scale when you read the book.

1. You know how to let go of the things that don't elevate your life or serve you.

> 1…...2…...3…...4…...5…...6…...7…...8…...9…...10
> *<I hold onto everything   I'm free!>*

2. You're not highly critical of yourself or others. You positively impact people.

> 1…...2…...3…...4…...5…...6…...7…...8…...9…...10
> *<I criticize everyone.   I look for ways to build others up>*

3. You take care of yourself (mind, body, heart, soul).

> 1…...2…...3…...4…...5…...6…...7…...8…...9…...10
> *<I do nothing for myself Self-care is a definite priority!>*

4. You're comfortable with who you are.

> 1…...2…...3…...4…...5…...6…...7…...8…...9…...10
> *<Not even close   Overflowing>*

5. You know your value.

> 1…...2…...3…...4…...5…...6…...7…...8…...9…...10
> *<Hideous   Gorgeous>*

6. You claim responsibility for your life.

1…...2…...3…...4…...5…...6…...7…...8…...9…...10
<Nothing is my fault   I own it!>

7. You are a contributor and bring joy with you wherever you go.

1…...2…...3…...4…...5…...6…...7…...8…...9…...10
<I am miserable   I'm full of joy!>

8. You create your own happiness and you do work that fulfills you.

1…...2…...3…...4…...5…...6…...7…...8…...9…...10
<What's happiness?   I jump out of bed each morning>

9. You are courageously yourself and live fully.

1…...2…...3…...4…...5…...6…...7…...8…...9…...10
<Total Scaredy-Cat   I'm my own Superhero!>

10. The only approval you need is your own.

1…...2…...3…...4…...5…...6…...7…...8…...9…...10
<I rely on others' opinions   I approve of me>

11. You forgive yourself and others quickly.

1…...2…...3…...4…...5…...6…...7…...8…...9…...10
<I'm a grudge holder   I'm very forgiving>

12. You have healthy boundaries.

1…...2…...3…....4…....5…....6…....7…....8…....9…....10
<*Others walk all over me.*
  I'm definite about what is acceptable and communicate that.>

13. You lead your life from intention, not from competition.

1…...2…...3…....4…....5…....6…....7…....8…....9…....10
<*I will win no matter what   Intention fuels me*>

14. If something doesn't work, you shift it, not suffer it!

1…...2…...3…....4…....5…....6…....7…....8…....9…....10
<*I'm suffering   I'm happy beyond words*>

On the joy scale, which numbers are lower than you'd like? Note those as we carry on in this section as we start to uncover some of our main challenges.

_____

_____

_____

_____

_____

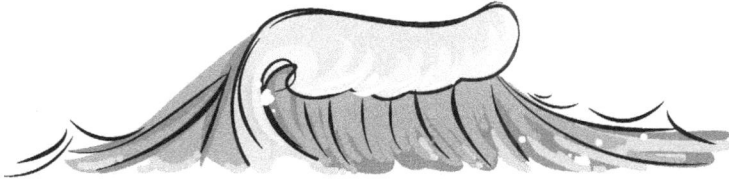

"Where focus goes, energy flows."
- Richard Janes

Now we want to prioritize the realms of our lives where we want to boost joy.

First, you'll rank the realms by their importance to you. That will help you select your top 3. If you're not sure right away, a good place to start is with those areas that weigh on you, where you feel stuck, or where there isn't good flow. Rank each one on a scale of 1 to 11, with 1 being least important right now and 11 being most important. While each of these realms is important, you'll pare your focus down to three that are the most important now.

Here are some areas to consider. Pick 3.

____ Realm 1: Love and relationships (intimate & family)

____ Realm 2: Friends, community & home life

____ Realm 3: Work life, passions, career and finances

____ Realm 4: Health and well-being

____ Realm 5: Mindset and Spirituality

Of the realms, pick three you want to dive into right now and clarify what the main challenge is that needs a joy infusion!

Realm One: _____

Main Challenge: _____

Realm Two: _____

Main Challenge: _____

Realm Three: _____

Main Challenge: _____

TAKE ACTION - Week Seven:

Feel free to journal anything that comes to you.

_____

_____

_____

_____

_____

_____

_____

_____

_____

_____

Congratulations! You've made it through lucky week seven.
For a bonus video, visit
www.marylpetreccia.com/workbookbonus

Module 8

The Joy Activation Process Technology

"Just follow your joy. Always. I think that if you do that, life
will take you on the course that it's meant to take you."
—*Jonathan Groff*

Now I want to introduce you to the best tool in your personal toolbox to elevate your life in a snap, the Joy Activation Process. To begin, look at last week's work about your top three realms and the main challenge for each.

The power of the Joy Activation Process is that it guides you to new choices and new actions.

The steps in the Joy Activation Process include:
·   Awaken
·   Acknowledge
·   Act
·   Adapt
·   Affirm

Basically, you take your challenge through the Joy Activation Process, clarify what you want instead and uncover new actions to get you there.

Awaken

Step one in the process, **Awaken**, is designed to shed light on your challenge so that you can articulate what you want instead. It's about what there is to take on right now and upgrade. As an aside, if you're feeling stuck or lost, that's actually perfect because now you can chart something new. Navigating new horizons starts with being "lost."

A tip before you get started: consider what you could release that is no longer serving you. It makes a big difference because whatever is stumping you—mindsets, attitudes, ideas, thoughts, or beliefs—releasing them makes way for new actions.

1) Pick one (and only one) challenge to work on so you can get the process down. Don't worry. You can use the process on every challenge you have, just one at a time.

_____

_____

_____

_____

2) Considering that challenge, what do you want instead? Put another way, what would be a better outcome to what you have now?

_____

_____

_____

_____

3) What's in the way? Assess the gap between what's challenging you and what you want instead. **List the roadblocks.** Roadblocks can be emotions, confidence, beliefs, thoughts, or myths we tell ourselves, mindsets, money, time, etc. In other words, what's stopping you from having what you want?

→ _____

→ _____

→ _____

→ _____

4) What is missing? To get beyond those roadblocks, what would you need to get, secure, take on that you don't have right now?

_____

_____

_____

_____

5) For something new to emerge, what would you need to say goodbye to?

_____

_____

_____

_____

_____

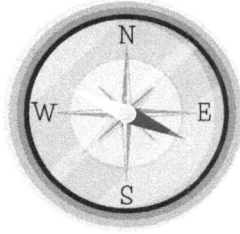

TAKE ACTION - Week Eight:

Use the journaling prompts below to work on what you saw above. Feel free to make changes based on what you see as you journal.

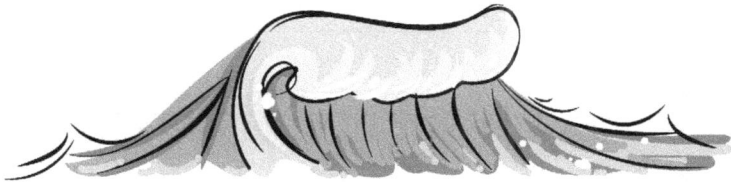

Day 1 Journaling: What are ways that you could change your interactions with other people to achieve the life you want? List them here.

➔ _____

➔ _____

➔ _____

➔ _____

➔ _____

➔ _____

➔ _____

➔ _____

➔ _____

➔ _____

➔ _____

➔ _____

➔ _____

Day 2 Journaling: What is scary about change for you? Do you worry about losing something?

_____

_____

_____

_____

_____

_____

_____

_____

_____

_____

Day 3 Journaling: What do you find exciting about change?

_____

_____

_____

_____

_____

_____

_____

_____

_____

_____

_____

Day 4 Journaling: What would your life look like if you had what you said you wanted in this week's exercise? Imagine you have exactly what you want. See it in your mind's eye in as much detail as possible.

_____

_____

_____

_____

_____

_____

_____

_____

_____

_____

_____

Day 5 Journaling: Write down single words or phrases that describe your new life. (For example, joy, time for friends, fun with the kids, alone time, freedom, happiness, peace of mind, etc.)

_____

_____

_____

_____

_____

_____

_____

_____

_____

_____

Day 6 Journaling: Who else would be impacted if you had what you said you wanted and how?

_____

_____

_____

_____

_____

_____

_____

_____

_____

_____

_____

Day 7 Journaling: Free day. Take some time. Write what comes to you.

_____

_____

_____

_____

_____

_____

_____

_____

_____

_____

Module 9

Acknowledge and Act

> *"Joy is the holy fire that keeps our purpose warm and our intelligence aglow."*
>
> *- Helen Keller*

In this module we will look at the next two steps of the Joy Activation Process: **Acknowledge and Act**.

Even though it's a new week, we are working with the same challenge that you identified in the previous week.

ACKNOWLEDGE

This step has us look at the impact of that specific challenge on our life as it stands now. Review the challenge to answer the questions below.

<u>Acknowledge</u>: In this section, write about the real impact of your challenge in detail.

The impact on my life is: (Example: *I'm down, not happy, feeling stuck, it sucks, like I'm a victim, I'm resigned about it, I haven't had a relationship for over a year, etc.*)

_____

_____

I am suffering. Here's how: (Example: *I've put on weight and don't care, I'm not as close to my kids and that's really hard, I'm afraid to open my mail, I don't want to talk to anybody, there's no point, etc.*)

_____

_____

_____

_____

_____

_____

Is there something about this issue that you just don't want to deal with? Is there an expectation you have that's not being met?

_____

_____

_____

_____

_____

_____

Act: NOW Actions vs. NEW Actions:

Every action moves you toward something. So, in this section, we are going to look at what your NOW actions are moving you towards which is easy because it's what you have now. And, we will look at what NEW actions will move you toward what you want.

Are your current actions moving you toward joy or away? What would you do instead, if anything?

NOW: What actions are you taking now? (Non-action is ALSO an action.) (Identify 1-3 or as many as you want.)

→ _____

→ _____

→ _____

What, if anything, do you notice about how your NOW actions are causing suffering on that issue?

_____

_____

_____

_____

_____

_____

NEW: What new actions could you take to get you to what you want? (Identify 1-3 or any number you want.)

→ _____

→ _____

→ _____

Now, we will decide what actions you will KEEP, MODIFY, or REPLACE.

NOW Action	KEEP, MODIFY or REPLACE	NEW Action

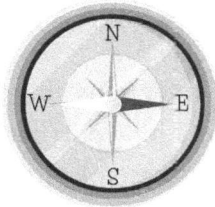

TAKE ACTION - Week Nine:

Where do intentions and actions intersect?

Intentions are identified actions designed to reach or produce a particular outcome (planning, forethought). Intentions are powerful declarations because they bring focus to a specific goal. The qualities of an intention are clarity and resolve to getting what you want.

Off the top of your head, what is an intention you would like to create this week?
What about this month and this year?

Just for fun, write them down and consider what would be involved for you to get that.

This Week	This Month	This Year

When you place your intentions in your visual field (like a note on the refrigerator, by your bed, bathroom mirror, or even as your cell phone screen,) oftentimes, that's enough to give them momentum. When they catch your eye, just ponder them for a few moments and let it go. My favorite is intention is: I CHOOSE TO GENERATE ABUNDANCE AND CONTRIBUTION IN EVERY INTERACTION.

In your journaling, you can write about how it makes you feel to see your intentions everywhere you look. At the end of the week, put the note (or picture on your phone) somewhere safe. Put a reminder on your phone 3 times a day to get present to your current intention for 2 weeks.

Day 1 Journaling: How do you feel just putting your
intentions or goals on paper?

_____

_____

_____

_____

_____

_____

_____

_____

Day 2 Journaling: What did you feel when you walked past the note today?

_____

_____

_____

_____

_____

_____

_____

_____

_____

_____

_____

Day 3 Journaling: Do you feel like your intentions and goals are more or less achievable than on day 1 this week?

_____

_____

_____

_____

_____

_____

_____

_____

_____

_____

_____

_____

Day 4 Journaling: What is one small step you could take toward one of your intentions or goals? Map it out with time it would take, money, etc.

_____

_____

_____

_____

_____

_____

_____

_____

_____

_____

_____

_____

Day 5 Journaling: Go for it - Take a small step toward your goal or intention today and write about it here.

_____

_____

_____

_____

_____

_____

_____

_____

_____

_____

_____

_____

Day 6 Journaling: Can you take another step, or go a little further? Do the next thing and write about it here.

_____

_____

_____

_____

_____

_____

_____

_____

_____

_____

_____

Day 7 Journaling: How do you feel after mapping out and acting on some small actions toward a goal?

_____

_____

_____

_____

_____

_____

_____

_____

_____

_____

You've made it over half way through. You're doing great. Keep going. For a bonus on acknowledging and acting go to www.gpstojoybook.com/bonuses

Maryl Petreccia

Module 10

Adapt and Affirm

"Sometimes your joy is the source of your smile, but sometimes your smile can be the source of your joy."
—*Nhat Hanh*

There is more than adjusting your actions. You also will want to define a plan and allow time for that plan to make a difference in the challenge you have identified. Anchor new actions by giving them three to four weeks to make an impact on your issue.

Adapt

What adjustments would you be ok with making so that the new actions can stick? You need to allow for it to work.

Anchor new actions by allowing 3-4 weeks for them to make an impact on your issue. Write your specific new action(s) and the timeframe you are allowing yourself to absorb those actions. Note them on your calendar for tracking your experience.

1)_____

_____

2)_____

_____

3)_____

_____

Also, as part of the Adapt step, I'd like you to read over the 13 practices below to navigate your joy. Circle up to three that would make the most difference in your ability to face the challenge. These habits bring fuel to the process.

1. You let go of the things that no longer serve you.
2. You're not highly critical of yourself or others.
3. You have routines that nurture you.
4. You're comfortable with yourself and you know your value.
5. You claim responsibility for your life.
6. You contribute often.
7. You create your own happiness and do what fulfills you.
8. You have the courage to be yourself and live fully.
9. The only approval you seek is your own.
10. You forgive yourself and others quickly.
11. You have healthy boundaries.
12. You lead your life from intention and what's possible.
13. If something is not working, you shift it.

The last step in the process involves affirming the new actions you have taken to improve outcomes on the challenge(s) you are facing. It's so rich and important to affirm ourselves and our actions as part of celebrating ourselves and our results. The joy this brings is palpable!

The following questions will cover Adapting and Affirming:

1) Developing a personal motto is also part of the Adapt step of the Joy Activation Process. What is your motto?
(Mine is - I AM BECOMING THE WOMAN OF MY DREAMS EVERY DAY.)

_____

_____

_____

2) How does your motto relate to the three habits above you circled?

_____

_____

_____

3) Name at least one specific task or time in your life that the habits you circled above would have caused you to take a different direction or make a different choice?

_____

_____

_____

_____

4) Check in and write about how the new actions are giving you a better outlook on your issue.

_____

_____

_____

_____

_____

_____

5) In what realms is life really working? Own it here! List one to three realms in which life is working well.

_____

_____

_____

_____

6) Write down up to three circumstances that are right where you want them:

_____

_____

_____

_____

_____

_____

_____

TAKE ACTION - Week Ten:

Adapting to new habits and new outcomes takes time. In the last module we mapped out a goal. This week, I want you to adapt all of the rest of your goals including the steps it will take, timing, and financials needed, if any, to accomplish those goals. Take your time with this. If you need support with it, reach out to me and join our facebook group. Please enjoy this process and make this mapping out your task for this week. Your future lies right here inside of this.Take as long as it needs, but also know that you will adapt these plans as you go.

Day 1 Journaling: How do you feel about writing out all of your steps for your tasks?

_____

_____

_____

_____

_____

_____

_____

Day 2 Journaling: Even if they aren't finished yet, how do you feel about task mapping today?

_____

_____

_____

_____

_____

_____

_____

_____

_____

_____

_____

Day 3 Journaling: Are you having feelings of "Why didn't I do this yet?" Write about those feelings here:

_____

_____

_____

_____

_____

_____

_____

_____

_____

Affirm yourself for being in action. Read the following statement and add your own affirmation(s) to it:

"I am regularly taking actions to face my challenges and am willing to keep on learning and growing and living my life from my dreams and what I desire, ***ONE CHOICE AT A TIME.***"

Day 4 Journaling: How do you feel after saying this affirmation?

_____

_____

_____

_____

_____

_____

_____

_____

Day 5 Journaling: What is a new affirmation you can add today?

_____

_____

_____

_____

_____

_____

_____

_____

_____

_____

Day 6 Journaling: Remember back a few weeks ago, when you made a "me monument?" Walk past that and write about how you feel about those things now.

_____

_____

_____

_____

_____

_____

_____

_____

_____

_____

_____

Day 7 Journaling: Does it feel like you're getting closer or further away and why?

_____

_____

_____

_____

_____

_____

_____

_____

_____

_____

_____

Module 11

Joy's Reference Points

"Let go of your attachment to being right, and suddenly your mind is more open. You're able to benefit from the unique viewpoints of others without being crippled by your own judgment."

- Ralph Marston

Now that you more fully understand the steps in the Joy Activation Process —Awakening, Acknowledging, Acting, Adapting, and Affirming—it's time to cover the reference points you can use to keep yourself on a joyful course. I'll outline the reference points or "bedrocks of joy" that provide a foundation and context to get joy flowing. These, in a nutshell, are my fundamental values—the coordinates of my G.P.S. to Joy—and they work hand-in-hand with the Joy Activation Process. When I honor my values, I experience joy.

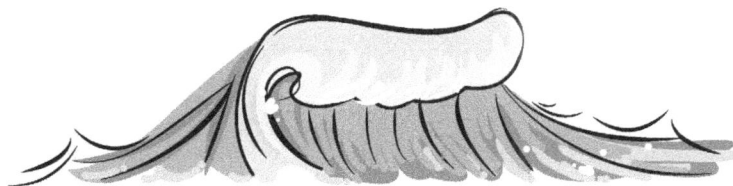

1) What transitions have you made so far? Do they feel big or small?

_____

_____

_____

_____

_____

2) Are you more or less likely to go with the flow? Why or why not?

_____

_____

_____

_____

_____

3) What sparks small happiness for you?

_____

_____

_____

_____

_____

_____

4) Where/what in your life still needs triage?

_____

_____

_____

_____

_____

_____

5) What expectations do you feel like you're failing? What are you surpassing?

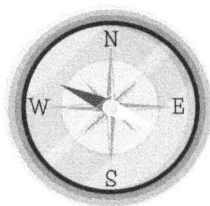

_____

_____

_____

_____

_____

_____

TAKE ACTION - Week Eleven:

Find a tiny thing you can do, preferably daily, for self care. It could be a hot chocolate, it could be taking five minutes to stretch, it could be going to bed an hour early and muting devices and reading a book or any other thing you've been desiring to do for yourself for a while. Set a specific time to do it, AND if you feel the desire to do it any other time of day, stop and take a moment to do it. Even if it's just a 30 second deep breath it counts as self-care.

Day 1 Journaling: What was the thing you did today for yourself? What are your feelings about it?

_____

_____

_____

_____

_____

_____

_____

_____

_____

_____

_____

Day 2 Journaling: What was the thing you did today for yourself? Did it feel better or weirder than yesterday?

Day 3 Journaling: If you haven't already, do a different small thing for yourself that creates your joy zone today. What is changing?

_____

_____

_____

_____

_____

_____

_____

_____

_____

_____

Day 4 Journaling: Where are you finding your joy flow today?

_____

_____

_____

_____

_____

_____

_____

_____

_____

_____

_____

_____

Day 5 Journaling: What magic would you like to see or feel today?

_____

_____

_____

_____

_____

_____

_____

_____

_____

_____

_____

Day 6 Journaling: Do two things today that you find joy in. Does it feel good or gratuitous? Why?

_____

_____

_____

_____

_____

_____

_____

_____

_____

_____

_____

_____

Day 7 Journaling: Is finding joy getting easier for you? Why or Why not?

_____

_____

_____

_____

_____

_____

_____

_____

_____

_____

Maryl Petreccia

144

Module 12

Where Is Your Joy G.P.S. Telling You to Go Next?

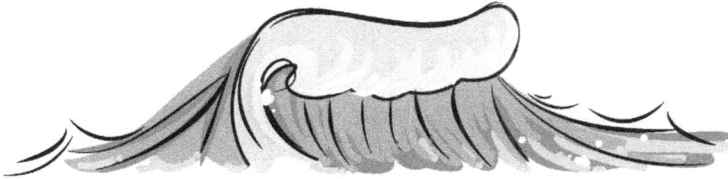

"There are those who give with joy, and that joy is their reward."
—*Khalil Gibran*

1) When is your joy flow easy to maintain? When is it hard?

_____

_____

_____

_____

_____

_____

2) Where are you in the steps to reaching your goals? Do you need to remap?

_____

_____

_____

_____

_____

3) Flip back to module one and look at your answers. How do you feel about those answers?

_____

_____

_____

_____

_____

4) Does Joy feel hard or awkward? Why?

_____

_____

_____

_____

_____

_____

5) How is your mantra helping you? (If it's not strong enough, write a new one here!)

_____

_____

_____

_____

_____

_____

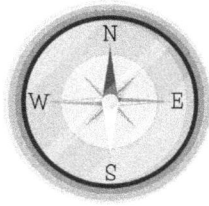

TAKE ACTION - Week Twelve:

Day 1 Journaling: **Open your heart and Get joyful:** Ignite your joy with whatever stirs your soul, like music, art, sewing, acting, gardening, etc. My heart-opener is dancing. Journal about what you do.

_____

_____

_____

_____

_____

_____

_____

Day 2 Journaling: **Self-care:** This seems like the first thing to go! We are so used to putting everything else first before our own bodies! But ignoring our bodies keeps joy in the shadows. Take a day off, plan a vacation, sleep late, take a long walk or bath. Write about it here:

_____

_____

_____

_____

_____

_____

_____

_____

_____

_____

Day 3 Journaling: **Movement:** I dance, do yoga, take walks on the beach, and train for strength—all to keep the flow of joy active in my body. As we strengthen our bodies, we expand ourselves for joy. What are you doing to keep your body strong and healthy?

Day 4 Journaling: **Compulsion clarity:** Get as clear as you can about your fears and anxieties because they are making decisions for you! What are you still feeling fearful or anxious about?

_____

_____

_____

_____

_____

_____

_____

_____

_____

_____

Day 5 Journaling: **Your non-negotiables:** Have you thought about boundaries that need redefining because it's just that time in your life? What are your non-negotiables?

Day 6 Journaling: **Space for the new to emerge:** I listen to the ocean outside my bedroom window and the singing birds in my garden. I breathe deeply, all the way to my toes. I meditate and pray words of gratitude. I practice yoga, forgiveness, and much more. Find your way to make space daily where you can. What space are you creating? How can you create even more?

_____

_____

_____

_____

_____

_____

_____

_____

_____

Day 7 Journaling: **Connect to love everywhere:** Feel love for yourself, for your source, for your community. Notice love both internally and outside in your world, as one mirrors the other. There is no right place to start. Connect right where you are. Where and who are you connecting with?

_____

_____

_____

_____

_____

_____

_____

_____

_____

_____

Final Thoughts

Activating your joy is not a destination. It's an on-going adventure! The compass we use is our mindset, and it gives us a context that helps us lay a solid foundation for the future we want to attract.

I now know that we can experience ourselves from our visions and dreams **now**. The only real gap between now and the future we want is self-imposed limits. Embracing growth is part of the practice that allows us to expand in our thinking and widening our heart space where love and joy becomes palpable, like the beating of our hearts.

Joy is not fickle and elusive. Joy is always present and simply asks for our awareness. Are you ready to activate your joy? That you can do right now, simply by being present and connected to your heart.

Stay true to your pursuit of a joy driven life! Start each day as if it's what you have to work with. Go back or forward - there is no wrong direction. Just keep on taking on the weekly actions and journaling. Whatever you do, keep going. You've started this journey and have turned it into a miraculous adventure. I am so happy you're here that I could literally jump right off of this page and give you the BIGGEST hug! I wish you love and might and look forward to getting to know you as we expand joy together in The Joy Continuum! Please reach out any time and visit the website to let me know how you're doing!

In joy,

Maryl Petreccia, #joyexpert
www.marylpetreccia.com
@activateyourjoy
www.gpstojoybook.com

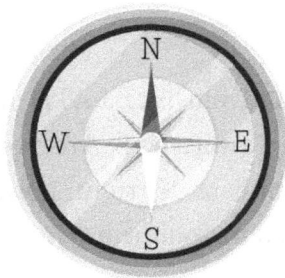